C000098578

Teen People PRESENTS

Prince WILLIAM

PRINCE OF HEARTS

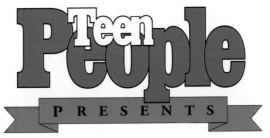

Prince WILLIAM

PRINCE OF HEARTS

Lisa Degnen

WARNER BOOKS

A Time Warner Company

If you purchased this book without a cover you should be aware that this book may have been stolen property and reported as "unsold and destroyed" to the publisher. In such case neither the author nor the publisher has received any payment for this "stripped book."

Copyright ©1998 by Michael Friedman Publishing Group, Inc. All rights reserved.

Warner Books, Inc., 1271 Avenue of the Americas, New York, NY 10020

Visit our Web site at http://warnerbooks.com

 A Time Warner Company

TEEN PEOPLE is a trademark of Time Inc., used with permission.

Printed in the United States of America

First Printing: December 1998

10 9 8 7 6 5 4 3 2 1

Library of Congress Cataloging-in-Publication Data
ISBN: 0-446-67539-3
LC: 98-86955

Editor: Emily Zelner
Art Director: Jeff Batzli
Designer: Millie Sensat
Photography Editor: Jennifer L. Bove
Production Manager: Camille Lee

Front cover photography: ©Anwar Hussein/All Action/Retna
Back cover photography: ©Camerapress/Retna

ONTENTS

INTRODUCTION

The eyes of the world are on Prince William, the future King of England. His Royal Highness William Arthur Philip Louis is currently second in line to inherit the British throne. His father, Charles, Prince of Wales, is the next in line to be King. Charles's mother, Queen Elizabeth, is Britain's current monarch.

The expectations are high for the future King William V. In 1981, when Prince Charles married Lady Diana Spencer, the British public waited anxiously for Charles to conduct himself in a more traditional style as heir to the constitutional monarchy and for Diana to assume a popular place among the people. The failure of the royal marriage, however, shattered that hope and eventually diminished the public's recognition of the monarchy. Young Prince William has a hefty weight resting on his shoulders and some pretty big shoes to fill. The hope of the British

people lies in his ability to rise to the occasion when he inherits the throne of England to become the leader for whom Britain has been waiting.

Thus far, he's done an admirable job of winning the hearts and favor of the public. In fact, he has a fan club that extends across the globe, as far as Canada, the United States, and Australia. When William visited Canada in March 1998, he was warmly greeted by crowds of screaming teenage girls waving signs that expressed their affection for the young prince. "William is intelligent and great fun," says one friend. "But the best thing about him is that he has a good and generous heart." William's fans are growing stronger in number every day. "This is the first time a member of the royal family has been popular with teenagers," says British editor Jeremy Mark. "They see him as a regular boy growing up in Britain."

Opposite: Already as photogenic as his beautiful mother, two-year-old William posed for formal photos before his brother Harry's christening in 1984.
Right: Blond, blue-eyed, tall, and handsome, William is a teen idol at sixteen years of age.

CHAPTER I
GROWING UP

William was born on June 21, 1982, to Prince Charles Philip Arthur George and Diana, Princess of Wales. A healthy baby boy weighing in at 7 pounds, 10 ounces (3.4kg), his birth was the cause of national celebration, with the succession to the British throne now ensured. Charles and Diana severed an ancient royal tradition when they decided to raise William themselves rather than having him reared solely by nannies. They changed his diapers, fed him and bathed him; in short, they appropriated responsibilities that members of the royal family had customarily deemed the duties of the nannies. When he was just a baby, the young prince traveled with his parents to Australia and New Zealand. These are just a

few of the ways that Charles and Diana broke with royal tradition when it came to William's upbringing.

As a toddler, William could be quite a handful, which earned him a number of nicknames, including King Tot, Billy the Basher, and William the Terrible! He was often found climbing into wastebaskets, attempting to flush dad's shoes down the toilet (when he was not filling the empty shoes with golf balls) and curiously pressing buttons, which often led to alarms ringing around Buckingham Palace. His behavior was not particularly unusual for a child of his age, but he was a royal toddler, and that made all the difference. For all the mischievous antics that the press naturally latched onto, William had his share of heartwarming moments, which were also recorded

Opposite: Radiant new mother Diana posed with baby
William in the White Drawing room of Buckingham Palace
on the day of his christening, August 4, 1982. This was also
the date of the Queen Mum's eighty-second birthday—truly
a royal celebration! **Below:** Charles and Diana pose with
baby William in one of their first family portraits.

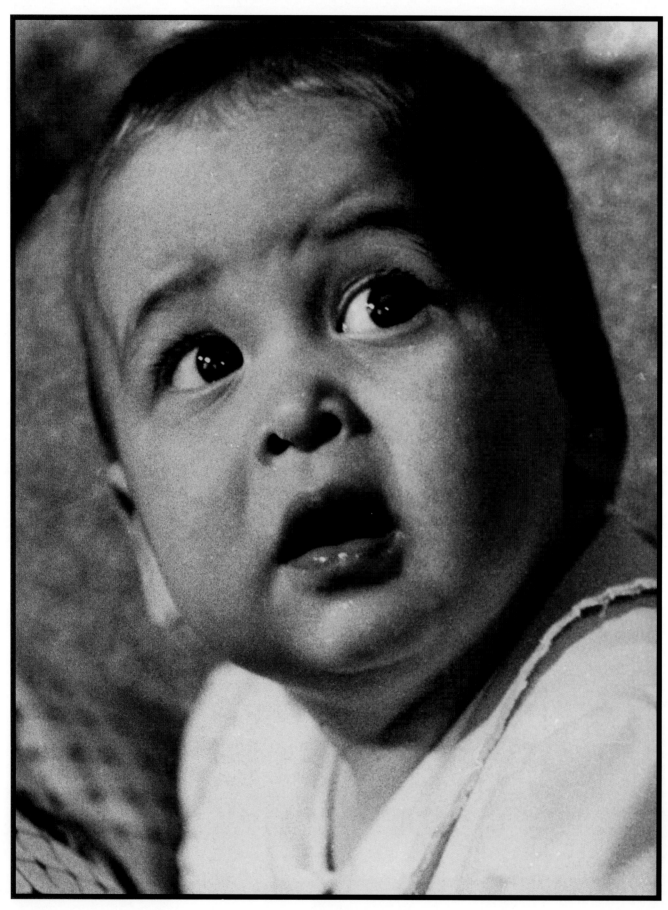

Prince
WILLIAM

Opposite: Prince William posed for his first photo session when he was six months old. "He was a lovely little boy who has grown up to be a very handsome young man," says a royal writer.

Above: Prince Charles and Princess Diana play with their son at Kensington Palace in 1982. The little prince wore a white silk romper with embroidery on the chest. **Left:** Prince Charles was beaming when he posed with his new son at Kensington Palace.

for the world to read about in the news and see in photographs. He was both nurturing and playful with little brother, Harry, and the brothers were known to cuddle when Harry was just a baby. William had mastered a handshake and a salute by age three and by age four he was excitedly waving to cameras while he took a ride on his pony, Trigger. Gradually the wild little boy grew into the self-assured young man that he is today. At age eleven, William spoke about wanting to grow up and become a police officer. But in his heart, he knew that he would grow up to serve 270 million subjects as the King of England.

Diana carefully trained William and her second son, Harry, to appreciate their public duties, but also to make the most of their private time. For this reason, the Princess instituted "fun days" and "work days." On "fun days," the boys could dress in jeans and baseball caps, go to McDonald's for lunch, watch a movie, and even ride on a roller coaster. On "work days" the Princes would have to attend to their royal duties—they would be required to dress in suits and ties, shake hands with the public and "forget any thoughts of selfishness." This would help them to understand the demands that lay ahead of them in life.

Right: Diana and Charles took William out for a family picnic during a visit to New Zealand in 1983. He posed for photographs and demonstrated his ability to crawl for the photographers. **Opposite:** Prince William at ten months. Even with only a few teeth, he already had that winning smile!

Prince
WILLIAM
16

William was the first royal baby to travel with his parents. The young prince accompanied them to Australia and New Zealand when he was nine months old.

Left: William adored all of the attention he got from photographers at Kensington Palace when he was just seventeen months old. But all that would change as he got older. "William has a hard time with public exposure," one royal watcher says of the future King. **Opposite:** William plays ball outside Kensington Palace on his second birthday. As a teenager, he would become a huge soccer fan.

Prince
WILLIAM
20

Below: It was a serious young boy who walked into Mrs. Mynor's Nursery School in 1985, but it didn't take long for William to become the most popular kid in class.

Above: William braved the rain to cheer on his dad at a polo match in 1987. **Opposite:** His family nicknamed William "Willy the Wombat" when he was still a tiny boy.

Life in the spotlight. Little William had photographers
following him everywhere. Even the sight of him riding his
bike across the palace yard became a media event.

"His Royal Sighness" takes his first ride on a horse. Actually it was just a pony, but it was still serious business for the future King.

Prince
WILLIAM
24

Opposite: William has known his own mind ever since he was a little boy, and friends say he can be quite stubborn when he wants to. "He doesn't like the idea of being pushed into anything," says royal watcher Ingrid Seward.

Above: Being a prince has its perks. William got to play soldier for the day in full uniform when he was only five years old.

Left: Six-year-old William and four-year-old Harry on the steps of Marivent Palace in Palma, Majorca, in 1988. The two princes and their parents spent their summer break with King Juan Carlos and Queen Sophia of Spain.

Right: One of the many privileges of royal life is getting to wear different hats. William once said he wanted to grow up to be a policeman—it looks like King will just have to do. **Opposite:** The press once dubbed them "The Heir and The Spare," but William and Harry have grown up to be the closest of brothers and since their mother's death, their bond has grown even stronger.

William and Harry gave a royal salute from atop a new motorcycle. Grown-up now, the two boys still love nice cars and fast motorcycles—just like boys anywhere in the world.

As important members of the royal family, William and
Harry had to learn to be independent at a very young age.
In 1991, they traveled on the royal yacht from England to
Canada and arrived the day before their parents.
Here they pose with Rear Admiral Robert Woodard
onboard the *Britannia*.

Right: Four-year-old William and two-year-old Harry share an umbrella at a polo match in 1987. William, always the protective older brother, shields Harry from the rain.

Opposite: Animals are a regular part of the sporting life for William and Harry. They hunt regularly, assisted by dogs and horses.

In March of 1991, Prince William was excused from school at Ludgrove to fulfill his first official royal engagement. He traveled with his mother to Cardiff, Wales, where he unveiled a new plaque.

Wearing yellow daffodils in honor of St. David's Day—the national holiday of Wales—Prince William and Princess Diana attended to their royal duties.

Below: Seven-year-old William worked the crowd like a pro during his first official engagement in Cardiff. He shook countless hands, smiling and greeting a crowd of over 2,500.

Opposite: There were hints of what was to come during William's first day on the job. He blushed when he was handed a bouquet of flowers, and again when a woman leaned over the barricades to kiss him.

Prince William's Education

When it came to William's schooling, Charles and Diana were determined to make the experience as mainstream as possible, keeping in line with their overarching views about his upbringing. They did not want him to receive private tutoring, as Charles had as a youngster. Rather, they were interested in seeing him interact with other children and allowing him to develop emotionally and socially in a largely conventional setting.

When Prince William attended his very first day of nursery school in West London, about a thousand photographers followed his every movement. William looked absolutely adorable wearing his red shorts and carrying a Postman Pat lunchbox. Even though he had a team of security guards surrounding him, Wills still managed to make a friend. Together, Wills and his new pal, Nicholas, were a mischievous duo. They were known to go wild with the finger paints and they once even flushed another kid's lunch down the toilet!

After two years as a student at Mrs. Mynor's Nursery School, William went on to attend Wetherby, a school for boys ages four to eight in Kensington, London. Wetherby emphasized music and manners, and William certainly excelled there. It was during this time that he got the nickname Billy the Basher because he liked to play rowdy sports and organize football games.

At age eight, following the route of the traditional British school system, William started boarding school.

He attended Ludgrove, located about twenty-five miles (40km) outside London. There he boarded with four other boys, shared a bathroom, and went to bed every night at eight—just like everyone else. His peers called him William and tried to treat him like one of the guys. At Ludgrove he took the very competitive exams that eventually got him accepted into the prestigious Eton College school. William finished the exams at the top of his class.

In 1995, William spent his first day at Eton. He'll study there for five years before attending a university. Eton is an exclusive school known for its rigorous acade-

Opposite: William and Harry in their Wetherby School uniforms with Mum in 1989. Diana once joked that William will grow up with all the responsibility and Harry will get all the girls.

Right: Prince William on his first day at the Wetherby School in 1987. He had to wear the school uniform, which included regulation shorts, even in the middle of winter.

Above: Prince William was never afraid to become a part of the action when he played sports. During his first year at the Wetherby School, William was quick to join almost every activity.

Right: During "Sports Day" at Wetherby in 1989. Princess Diana was on hand to cheer on her young sports star.

mics and athletics. Its student body of 1,300 has a large number of boys from prominent families, which makes it a particularly good school for William. In many ways, the prince's time at Eton will be the most "normal" period in his life. William's living quarters at Eton are pretty modest. He has a small room with a twin bed, a night stand, and a small window. The one thing he has that the other students do not is a private bathroom—he is the future King of England, after all!

On an average day at Eton William gets up at seven, has breakfast at eight, goes to chapel at 8:30, and starts classes at nine. There's a biscuit (cookie) break at 11:25. He goes to class until 1:25 and then breaks for lunch. Sports follow lunch and then afternoon classes resume at four and continue until dinner. As to be expected, the classes are challenging. William is studying English, chemistry, physics, biology, history, math, French, Greek, Latin, and art. Although some insiders say that his mother had hopes of his attending Harvard, in the United States, it is more likely that when he graduates from Eton, William will attend one of the top universities in England—probably Cambridge.

William signed the entrance book at Eton College on his first day of school in 1995, while his brother and parents looked on. William is the first royal heir to attend the 500-year-old school.

Prince
WILLIAM
40

Opposite: William in his formal Eton attire. William has a whole list of rules he has to follow when he's out in public. Two of the big ones: he can't be seen smoking or kissing a girl.

Left: Eton has become a welcome refuge for William ever since his mother's death. Boys at the school have been told they will be expelled if they talk about him to the press, and he knows that behind these gates he can relax and be himself.

Right: The centuries-old halls of Eton College have become a haven for William, a place completely secluded from the media. His brother Harry began attending Eton in the fall of 1998.

William loves playing rugby, and is thrilled that his schoolmates allow him to be a regular guy on the field. "William is
a promising sportsman," says reporter Peter Archer.

WILLIAM'S FAMILY TREE

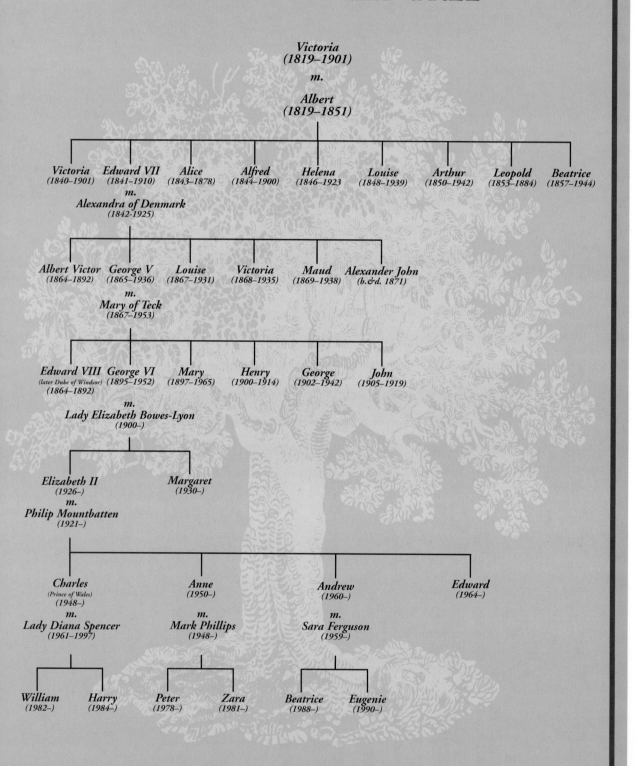

Victoria
(1819–1901)

m.

Albert
(1819–1851)

Victoria *(1840–1901)*	**Edward VII** *(1841–1910)*	**Alice** *(1843–1878)*	**Alfred** *(1844–1900)*	**Helena** *(1846–1923)*	**Louise** *(1848–1939)*	**Arthur** *(1850–1942)*	**Leopold** *(1853–1884)*	**Beatrice** *(1857–1944)*

m.

Alexandra of Denmark
(1842-1925)

Albert Victor *(1864–1892)*	**George V** *(1865–1936)*	**Louise** *(1867–1931)*	**Victoria** *(1868–1935)*	**Maud** *(1869–1938)*	**Alexander John** *(b.&d. 1871)*

m.

Mary of Teck
(1867–1953)

Edward VIII *(later Duke of Windsor)* *(1864–1892)*	**George VI** *(1895–1952)*	**Mary** *(1897–1965)*	**Henry** *(1900–1914)*	**George** *(1902–1942)*	**John** *(1905–1919)*

m.

Lady Elizabeth Bowes-Lyon
(1900–)

Elizabeth II *(1926–)*	**Margaret** *(1930–)*

m.

Philip Mountbatten
(1921–)

Charles *(Prince of Wales)* *(1948–)*	**Anne** *(1950–)*	**Andrew** *(1960–)*	**Edward** *(1964–)*

m. | m. | m.

Lady Diana Spencer *(1961–1997)* | **Mark Phillips** *(1948–)* | **Sara Ferguson** *(1959–)*

William *(1982–)*	**Harry** *(1984–)*	**Peter** *(1978–)*	**Zara** *(1981–)*	**Beatrice** *(1988–)*	**Eugenie** *(1990–)*

Prince
WILLIAM

William chats with his grandmother and great-grandmother

at the Queen Mum's birthday celebration in August 1995.

CHAPTER 2

REMEMBERING DIANA

William was especially close to Diana, and her tragic death in August 1997 was a momentous loss that he will have to deal with for the rest of his life. But friends say that William and Harry are handling the death of their mother with enormous courage. "Both boys are coping extremely well—perhaps better than anyone expected," a friend of Diana's told *People* magazine. "That tells you a lot about the royal blood. They have been taught from an early age that they have to present a certain facade."

Diana's friend Richard Branson says that William is very much like his beautiful mother. "The most wonderful thing is that Prince William has all the best attributes of Diana and she will live on through him," he says. Behind the scenes, one friend says that William's studies have suffered somewhat from his sadness. But the young prince is throwing himself into the regular routines by returning to school, and his house master at Eton, Dr. Andrew Gailey, and his wife are very supportive during this difficult time.

Left: Diana tried to teach William to cope with his public life and still enjoy his childhood. "The most wonderful thing is that Prince William has all the best attributes of Diana and she will live on through him," says media mogul Richard Branson. **Opposite:** Princess Diana's life was often difficult, but she loved every minute of motherhood.

Prince William was at his mother's side when they attended the Wimbledon Tennis Championships together in 1991. The two were very close. "William is sensitive and thoughtful, just like Diana was," a friend says. "Her spirit lives on through him."

Diana and Harry visit William at Eton. It was Diana's idea
to break with the rigid royal tradition of sending future
Kings to far away boarding schools in Scotland. Instead,
William is in England and near his family.

A Test of Courage

Everyone who knows William says that ever since his mother died, he has been brave beyond his years. From the moment he learned of his mother's sudden death in Paris, William assumed the role of the protective older brother. He was at Harry's side when they attended a private service at Crathie Church. And he was the one who made it clear that both he and Harry would prefer to be left to grieve alone at the family estate in Balmoral in Scotland.

It is known that William was upset when hordes of reporters and photographers showed up at Balmoral after Diana's death. He hates to be on display and being out in public during such an emotionally trying time was almost too much to bear. William had to be persuaded to appear in front of the cameras with his brother, father, grandmother, and grandfather.

Following the Princess's death, William received thousands and thousands of sympathy notes. Slowly, he has gotten used to all of the media attention and even managed to smile for the cameras when he appeared at celebrations for his grandmother's golden wedding anniversary. He has told friends that he feels safe when he's out in public with Charles because he feels that his father protects him from unwanted publicity.

Left: Diana spent her thirty-fourth birthday participating in a mother/son tennis tournament at Ludgrove. The Princess had declined an invitation to a huge society wedding in London to spend the day with her son.

Opposite: William was just nine years old when he visited the Canadian side of Niagara Falls with his mom and Harry. **Right:** William and Harry synchronized their watches when they attended a Veterans Day celebration with their mother. "She always used to say she wanted William to be happy, and it's quite clear she wanted him to be King," says Peter Archer.

The boys had a great time skiing with their mother in
Austria in 1991. It was around this time that his parents'
marriage began to fall apart and William became a comfort
to his devastated mother.

William, Harry, and Diana went white-water rafting in
Colorado in 1995. Diana liked to encourage the boys to do
normal, everyday activities—she was the first royal to take
her kids to McDonald's.

After Diana's death, William turned to his father for love and support. Prince Charles has often been described as cold and aloof, but those closest to the family say that he is a very caring and loving father. Charles calls his two sons "my darling boys" and says they will always come first in his life. He has arranged his busy schedule so that he can maximize the time he spends with his boys. And if there is a chance to travel with him, Charles will often invite his sons to come along, but he never puts too much pressure on them to go if they don't want to.

Keeping William and Harry's private lives off limits to the press since Diana's death has been a major priority for the family. Newspaper editors and photographers were asked to keep their distance unless they were covering an event with a scheduled photo opportunity, and the press has been surprisingly cooperative. In order to really escape, though, William likes to go duck hunting at dawn with his older cousin Peter Phillips on one of the Queen's estates. Peter, four years older than William, is said to have taken his cousin under his wing and is trying to help him through rough times by involving him in a lot of activities. Prince Charles seems to be trying hard to allow William the time he needs to be among his own friends and he has moved to a large apartment at York House so that he and the boys can have plenty of room when they are in London. Diana's sisters, Lady Jane Fellowes and Lady Sarah McCorquodale, speak to William and Harry on an almost daily basis. Friends and members of both the Spencer and Windsor families have provided tremendous support for the boys since Diana's death. The future is bound to have its difficult moments, but if William handles himself with the same grace as he has throughout undoubtedly the most difficult year of his life, he will always succeed.

William personally thanked members of the huge crowds who gathered to pay tribute to his mother outside of Buckingham Palace after Diana's death. Most onlookers were surprised and impressed by his poise and maturity given the traumatic nature of the events.

THE RING THAT REMINDS HIM OF HAPPIER TIMES

The one possession that belonged to his mother that William especially wanted to hold onto was the beautiful engagement ring that she wore even after her divorce. William has told friends that the ring is a reminder to him of the love his parents once shared and he will always keep it as a symbol of their love. The ring is a perfect oval blue sapphire surrounded by fourteen smaller diamonds and set in 18-carat white gold. "William wanted a permanent memento of Diana and the happiest times of his parents," said a royal source. "He believes that his father loved his mother very much when they got married and that this ring was a token of their love." Diana loved the ring for the same reasons and wore it up until her death. Part of her always loved Charles despite everything that happened between them."

The ring was made by the crown jewelers and was placed on Diana's finger when she became engaged to Charles on February 24, 1981. Millions of copies made their way to fingers around the world and the original is said to be worth millions today.

William and Diana: Kindred Spirits

Most of us can't imagine losing a beloved parent at the age of fifteen and having to make public appearances just days after the death—to put on a brave face and have to greet thousands of people on the street with a smile. But that's exactly what William had to do while the entire world watched him. William, Harry, and Charles went out on the street to greet and thank the thousands of people who turned up in London with flowers and candles to express their grief. It was William who insisted that he walk with his mother's funeral procession to the church. He was still a boy but expressing all the right qualities for a future King. "All my hopes are on William now," Diana said shortly before she died. "I think it's too late for the rest of the family. But William…I think he has it."

William has kept his mother's engagement ring as a special memento. He has told friends that the ring is a reminder to him of the love his parents once shared.

Below: Prince William, Prince Harry, and Prince Charles grieving on September 9, 1997, the day of Princess Diana's funeral. **Opposite:** It was William's idea to honor his mother by walking behind her coffin in the funeral procession. His grandfather, the Duke of Edinburgh; William; Diana's brother Earl Spencer; Prince Harry; and Prince Charles followed behind Diana's casket through the streets of London.

William and Diana were as close as any mother and son could be. Her relaxed and tender ways were in great contrast to the more formal behavior of the royal family. Diana wanted her children to have as normal an upbringing as possible, but she also knew that there would be tremendous pressures on William as he assumed his public role, and she encouraged him to talk to her about everything he was feeling. "Diana knew she'd never be Queen, but her tremendous influence will be apparent from now until he becomes King," remarked a royal watcher. "Together they will change the monarchy."

From the minute William was born, Diana, a former nursery school teacher, lavished William with love and attention. She refused to leave him alone with nannies when she had to travel with Charles. Eventually she insisted that William be allowed to go to the more relaxed Eton, as opposed to the stricter Gordonstoun school in Scotland where Charles was sent to "toughen up." And William always returned his mother's affections. Once, he even had to be restrained when he thought a photographer had offended his mother.

When she died, it seemed like William's life had been ripped apart. But her love and influence will always remain with him. "Make no mistake, even in death, Diana has more influence than Grace Kelly or John Kennedy did on the future of their sons and country,"

said author Harold Brooks-Baker. "Her legacy of love will continue with William all the way to the throne."

When Diana died she left behind $35.6 million. The majority of that money will be inherited by William and Harry—who will each receive $11 million in a trust fund that they cannot touch until they are twenty-five. Some $13.5 million will go to pay for estate taxes, and $83,000 went to Diana's longtime butler, Paul Burrell. Diana's wardrobe, wedding dress, and royalties from the use of her picture or name will go to raise money for the many charities with which she was involved.

Above: Millions of cards, flowers, and toys were brought to Buckingham Palace by well-wishers who wanted to express their love for Diana. **Opposite:** William, Harry, and Prince Charles examining the tributes of flowers and gifts that were left at Balmoral Castle in Scotland after Diana's death.

CHAPTER 3
HIS ROYAL SIGHNESS

People magazine once named Prince William one of the "50 Most Beautiful People in the World." His sun-streaked blond hair, warm eyes, and winning smile have melted millions of teenage hearts. Whenever magazines put William on the cover, they are swamped with fan letters to the future King. Many of the girls who write to William even sign their letters, "the next Mrs. Windsor." Newspapers in his hometown of London have nicknamed William "His Royal Sighness" because of his ability to make girls swoon. "Prince William is an international star on the level of Leonardo DiCaprio," says Christina Ferrari, the managing editor of *Teen People.* "Girls are attracted to his looks and his glamour, but also to the fact that he seems approach-

able and down-to-earth." When William went with his father and thirteen-year-old brother Harry on a ski vacation to Canada's Whistler Mountain, thousands of girls turned out to cheer for him. "William, will you marry me?" the girls screamed.

Standing tall at 6'1" (182.5cm), William is almost embarrassed by all of the attention that he receives. Instead of chasing girls, he is concentrating on other activities in his life. Even though he doesn't date much, William certainly does notice a pretty girl when she walks past him. "At Eton," says a pal, "the boys will walk past a pretty girl and pay a lot of attention to her. William certainly isn't outwardly flirty, but he will look and smile and what girl could resist that?"

Right: A fanciful computer simulation of William in full kingly regalia. Many royal watchers believe that Charles will never rule, and that William will become the next King. **Opposite:** Prince William was fifteen years old when he told his parents that he didn't want be the King of England. But a royal source says: "In his heart, William understands what's expected of him and he'll follow through with his duty to his country."

Canadian girls went wild when William made a trip to Vancouver, British Columbia, in March. He met his loyal subjects during a visit to the Burnaby Secondary School. "He is the best looking guy I have ever seen," one teary-eyed teenager said.

Fun-loving Prince Harry looks up to his older brother William. Sources say Harry thinks it's very funny that teenage girls go ga-ga for Will, and scream his name everywhere the two princes go.

William enjoyed an aerial tour of Maritime Park during his
visit to Vancouver.

That Hair, Those Eyes

Yes, it's plain to see, Prince William is undoubtedly the best-looking royal that anyone can remember. It certainly appears that William has inherited his good looks largely from his mother's side of the family. He has the hooded lids, sparkling blue eyes, and charming smile reminiscent of his mother.

William likes to keep his beautiful blond hair conservatively short, and that's good since the cut can show off his perfect ears! On the day of his birth, the Queen is said to have looked down on her new grandson and said, "Thank goodness he hasn't got ears like his father."

The Spencer family descended from the illegitimate offspring of King Charles II, and William is said to have more English royal blood than the Queen. The Spencers are also inclined to be artistic. William's maternal great-grandmother Margaret Baring was a brilliant violinist, and his grandfather, the late Earl Spencer, was a talented photographer. Prince Charles says that William has an intuitive feel for literature. Of the brothers, William tends to be thoughtful and expressive, while Harry is the wild daredevil. Diana's friend Carolyn Bartholomew remarked that William is like his mother: "intuitive, switched on and highly perceptive."

Left: William celebrated Christmas with his father in 1995. The two have become especially close since Diana's death. Like his father, he loves horses, dogs, and outdoor sports.
Opposite: Star-watchers say William is just as popular as Hollywood's reigning king of teenage hearts, Leonardo DiCaprio. Says William of the comparison, "I think he will find it easier to be the king of Hollywood than I shall being the King of England."

When William Met Cindy

What would you do if you suddenly met your dream idol? What would you say if His Royal Highness, Prince William suddenly walked through the front door and invited himself in for tea? If you said you would melt into a world of red-faced fluster, where none of your words would come out clearly or be understood, you actually have a lot in common with William. That's exactly what happened to him a few years ago when he had the opportunity to meet the woman of his dreams, supermodel Cindy Crawford.

William mentioned to his mother that he had a crush on the model, and the next thing he knew, Diana had invited Cindy over to tea. When Cindy arrived, she found herself alone with William and they chatted for a few minutes before Diana arrived. Diana could see that William was blushing and whispered to Cindy, "He's just like me; when he runs out of things to say, he just blushes." In 1995, Diana predicted the future for the shy and often blushing William. "Look at the press," Diana said. "William will be King, and this is what it will be like. Harry will end up getting all the girls."

Left: William may be camera shy, but he certainly has a great photogenic smile. **Opposite:** An outdoorsman like his father, Prince William has been hunting for years at the family estate of Sandringham. He also skis, rows, swims, and plays rugby.

PERSONAL STUFF

NAME: William Arthur Philip Louis Windsor
(When the prince was born, it took a few weeks for Charles and Diana to agree on a name for him. Charles liked Arthur and Diana liked William, so they eventually compromised. Philip and Louis are names from Charles' family and Windsor is the family name of Great Britain's royal house.)

REAL LAST NAME: Schleswig-Holstein-Sönderborg-Glücksburg-Saxe-Coburg-Gotha
(William descends from the royal line of Queen Victoria of the Saxe-Coburg-Saalfield family. Victoria married her first cousin, Prince Albert of Saxe-Coburg-Gotha and together they had nine children whose marriages, in conjunction with the next generation of marriages, allied the British royal house with those of Germany, Denmark, Russia, Greece, and Rumania.)

NICKNAMES: Wills, Billy, Wombat, Billy the Basher, and William the Terrible

PARENTS: Prince Charles and the late Princess Diana

SIBLING: Younger brother, Prince Harry

BIRTH DATE: June 21, 1982

BIRTH PLACE: St. Mary's Hospital, London

STAR SIGN: Gemini/Cancer

HAIR: Sandy blond

EYES: Blue

FAVORITE COLOR: Blue

HAND ORIENTATION: Left

FAVORITE FOODS: Burgers, fries, pizza, pasta, chocolate, veggies, and venison

FAVORITE DRINK: Coca-Cola

PET: A Labrador dog named Widgeon

FAVORITE SPORTS: William is a swimming champion at school. He won both the 100-meter and 50-meter freestyle races. He also likes hunting, skiing, tennis, soccer, hockey, and rafting.

WHERE YOU CAN WRITE TO HIM:

HRH Prince William
Kensington Palace
Kensington, London W8 4PN
Great Britain

HRH Prince William
St. James Place
London SW1A 1BS
Great Britain

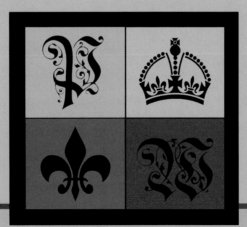

Opposite: Prince Charles, Harry, and William enjoying nature on a walk through the family estate at Balmoral in 1997.

Above: William at Balmoral. Balmoral was purchased by Prince Albert for Queen Victoria in 1852. To this day, it remains a favorite vacation getaway for the royal family.

THE WINDSOR FAMILY

Windsor is the family name of the royal house of Great Britain. George V changed the name from Wettin to Windsor in 1917 in order to make it sound less German. The name originated with Albert of Saxe-Coburg-Gotha, first cousin and husband of Queen Victoria. Two generations later in 1947, Queen Elizabeth II married Philip Mountbatten (né Schleswig-Holstein-Sönderborg-Glücksburg), who renounced his claim to the Greek throne, became a naturalized British citizen, and anglicized his name to Mountbatten when King George VI begrudgingly granted him permission to marry his daughter. In 1952, the Queen ruled that she and her decendants should keep the Windsor name. A decree of 1960 limited the name to the those descendants with the title prince or princess. Other descendants would carry the name Mountbatten-Windsor. So Prince William, as grandson of Queen Elizabeth II and Prince Philip, bears the name William Arthur Philip Louis Windsor.

To learn more about the royal family's lineage and succession to the British throne, visit the royal Website at www.royal.gov.uk, where you will find a family tree that dates back to 802.

The People in William's Life

It's not easy growing up to be the future King of England. William relies on a close group of friends and family to help make it through life's tough moments. Among his group of intimates:

Tiggy Legge-Bourke

Her real name is Alexandra, but all of her friends (including William and Harry) know her simply as Tiggy. Tiggy is very popular with both boys and she is usually seen laughing or smiling when she is with the two princes. William first came to know Tiggy when she was working as his nanny. Eventually both he and Harry grew too old to have a nanny and Tiggy left the palace. The boys have always remained in close contact with her, however, and she has frequently been by their side in the aftermath of Diana's death.

Peter Phillips

Peter is William's cousin (the son of Princess Anne, Charles's sister). William looks up to Peter as a sort of older brother and role model and has really come to rely on him since Diana died. They often meet to go hunting and to talk.

Left: William gets a visit at Eton from his former nanny Tiggy Legge-Bourke and his dog. Pals say William has often turned to Tiggy to help him cope with his mother's death. **Opposite, bottom:** Prince William's close relations and friends have helped him through difficult times. Here he is seen with both Peter Phillips and Tiggy Legge-Bourke in 1997.

Left: William walks to Christmas services at Sandringham Church with his cousin Peter Phillips in 1997. Peter is four years older than William and has become as close to him as an older brother.

Left: Prince William is also close to his cousin Zara Phillips, who, sources say, loves to tease him and make him blush.

Opposite: William is caught by cameras during his grandparents' fiftieth wedding celebration in 1997. When a magazine ran a cover story on him, William started getting more than 12,000 fan letters a week.

Above: William on his first day at Eton with his house-master, Dr. Andrew Gailey. Dr. Gailey has helped William through trying times, including his parents' divorce and his mother's tragic death. **Opposite:** William with Harry and his father at Balmoral. When they are at the Scottish estate, the threesome enjoy going on long hikes and hunting in the woods. William has been hunting with his father since he was just four years old.

Prince Harry

Born on September 18, 1984, Prince Harry (real name, His Royal Highness, Prince Henry of Wales) is probably the person closest to William, and undoubtedly the person who can bring a smile to his face the quickest. Harry is crazy about soccer (called football in England) and he loves to go to games with his friends. Since their mother's sad death, William and Harry have gotten even closer. When William and Harry aren't in school, they spend their days at their father's Highgrove country estate or his London apartment. Harry is known for his winning grin. They couldn't wipe that grin off his face when he got to meet the Spice Girls. Friends say he adores his older brother and would like to grow up to be just like him.

Prince Charles

Although Charles often gets called conservative and stuffy, William knows a different side of his father. "Charles can be fun-loving and loves to spend his days with the boys in the country," says a source. "William was absolutely devoted to his mother, but he loves his father, too." Recalling his own experiences growing up in the British royal family, Charles once confessed that he understood William's shyness and sympathized with William because of what lay ahead in his future.

Charles is the next in line to take over the throne from his mother, Queen Elizabeth, but William might actually jump ahead of him to be the next King. At the time of her death, Prince Charles was divorced from William's mother, Princess Diana. It is said that Charles really wants to marry his longtime companion, Camilla Parker-Bowles. If that happens, many people think the British public would prefer to see Prince Charles step aside and William ascend the throne. But until Queen Elizabeth's reign is over, the rest of the world will just have to wait and see what the future holds.

Prince
WILLIAM
78

Right: William enjoying a few minutes of quiet time alone on a hike in Scotland. The young prince enjoys his privacy. **Opposite:** William playing with his beloved dog, Widgeon, at Balmoral. There are over 50,000 acres of land at the estate, leaving lots of woodlands to roam and trails to hike.

Most of William's holidays with his father are spent enjoying the great outdoors. This family get-together at Balmoral
occurred just a month before Diana's death.

Prince
WILLIAM

Prince Charles shares a ski lift with William in Switzerland in 1993. He calls William "my darling boy" and spends as much time as possible with his son when he's not in school.

Six months after Diana's death, Prince Charles took William
and Harry on a ski vacation to Canada's Whistler Mountain.
William was a master of the mountain and a hit with
teenage girls throughout North America.

Left: Prince William and Prince Charles having a heart-to-heart talk on the ski lift in Klosters, Switzerland. Diana's tragic death has drawn Charles closer to his two sons.
Opposite: William has skied since he was very young, traveling with his parents to hit the slopes in places like Switzerland, Austria, and Colorado.

Prince
WILLIAM
85

DID YOU KNOW?

♣ William has tea with the Queen (also known as his granny) almost every Sunday.

♣ When he was just thirteen years old, William said he would not join the Royal Navy, despite the family tradition that saw his grandfather, his father and uncles before him all join up.

♣ Prince William loves to search the World Wide Web. He often sends e-mail to friends and family and he regularly corresponds electronically with the Queen. So the next time you're online, you might be secretly chatting with the future King of England!

♣ Despite what you might have heard, William does get a chance now and then to let his hair down with his friends. He has gone to discos in London (okay, he has to bring six bodyguards with him) and he's been known to party with schoolmates.

♣ One of William's closest friends is his cousin Peter Phillips, who is the son of his father's sister, Princess Anne. Peter was standing at William's side for most of Diana's funeral.

♣ His favorite pin-up girl is model Christie Brinkley.

♣ William likes to watch the British version of MTV. He loves many different types of music, but he is especially fond of Techno music. He likes the Spice Girls and he sometimes listens to Pulp or Oasis.

♣ William could marry an American girl if he wanted to, but she would have to be a Protestant who had never been divorced. The rule in England is that anyone in the direct line to the throne can not marry a Roman Catholic, because the ruler of the crown also holds the title of Defender of the Faith of the Church of England.

♣ There's a long list of things Prince William *can't* do—especially when he's in public. Among the things he's forbidden from doing: no drinking alcohol in public, no smoking or taking drugs, no kissing girls in public. Also, he can't be photographed inside a dance, he must stay with his bodyguards at all times, he has to go into and leave a party with his aides (not school friends), he has to be home by a certain hour, and he has to get permission before he goes to any disco or party.

Dating

When it comes to dating, there are rules, rules, rules. For example, kissing in public is a definite taboo. The palace has a great influence over which girls William is permitted to date. And when it comes time for marriage— well, that's another story!

When William was younger he liked a girl in Scotland named Marina, but he told his father he never got a chance to talk to her alone, because he always had a detective standing over his shoulder. Finally, Charles said that he would stay near William instead of the detectives.

"Oh all right," William said, "but stand at least twenty yards away, please!"

William has already gone on a few dates with some of his friends' sisters and the palace has carefully looked at all of them. "He can go out with the girls of his own choosing," says a palace insider, "but they'll obviously be from a suitable background, because those are the only girls he'll be allowed to meet. William is expected to keep the monarchy just as popular as Diana did when she was alive, so it will be a hard role for any girl he chooses to marry. He must choose very carefully."

For now, William is still young and shy, but no doubt interested in girls and dating. Already a teen idol across the world, he has a busy future ahead of him and no lack of young women who are more than aware of his good looks and eligibility!

Opposite: In December of 1997 William attended the *Spice World* premiere in London. **Left:** William is charming through and through. "He comes across quite sympathetically, as thoughtful and sensitive with an artistic flair," says British Press Association's Peter Archer.

At thirteen, William was a novice rower; now, he excels at
many sports. He also loves to read and go to the theater.

Sweet Sixteen

William's sixteenth birthday on June 21, 1998, was his first birthday without his mother. He wanted to make it a very quiet day with his pals from Eton and a few phone calls from his family. "He had a happy day and said a prayer for his mum," said a source. "He does think about her every single day. Probably a day will never go by when she doesn't pass through his thoughts."

Royal chefs baked him a big chocolate cake with sixteen candles. Radio stations throughout England, Scotland, and Wales played birthday wishes to William from listeners, and dedicated special tunes like Ringo Starr's "You're 16, You're Beautiful and You're Mine" to the young prince.

As part of an agreement with the British press to give him privacy most of the time, William agreed to answer a few questions about his personal life that the papers printed along with big full-page color posters of him. William revealed that when Princess Diana died in a car crash the summer before, he felt like his whole world fell apart.

William also answered questions about his interests and hobbies. He said that he loves computer games, but

Prince
WILLIAM

doesn't own a computer. He loves horses and his dog, Widgeon (named after a type of wild duck). He likes studying geography, biology, and art history, but he hasn't decided what he'll study once he goes to university. William spends a lot of his free time at school swimming. He entered a swimming race at Eton to raise money for a cancer charity and he has also done some other charity work with the boys at school. William is a double-swimming champion, winning junior awards at his school's 100-meter and 50-meter freestyle races, and he has been ranked among the top one hundred swimmers in Britain for his age. William also revealed that he is crazy for Techno music, although he wouldn't say who his favorite group is. One newspaper in England, the *Mirror*, gave a snooty explanation of Techno music: "It came from the U.S. underground. . . . It's hardly music at all."

The royal family also released school records revealing that both of his parents came to his school for various activities and that he acted in two school plays that were attended by both his parents and his brother. "Prince William was very popular with the other children and was known for his kindness, sense of fun and quality of thoughtfulness," says one school record.

William also told the press that it makes him a little uncomfortable to be a pin-up boy. "Sometimes he just doesn't understand all of the attention he's getting," says a friend. "He wants to be a normal guy."

IT'S IN THE STARS

What William's Horoscope Means

Born on June 21, 1982, William is a Gemini on the cusp of Cancer. Cusp babies are in the special position of sharing some of the qualities of both signs, so William has characteristics typical of both Gemini and Cancer. Interestingly, Princess Diana, who was born on July 1, was a Cancer.

His stars say that William is sensitive (a Cancerian trait he shares with Diana) and imaginative, a young man who sees the beauty in all things. He has a lively and curious mind, and enjoys trying new things. Indeed, Geminis, ruled by Mercury, are known for craving change and keeping up with the latest trends.

In love, William will prove affectionate, steadfast and loyal—not one to play around, once William falls in love with a girl, he'll be hers forever.

Although his mischievous sense of humor ensures that William is a fun date, his star profile also shows that the prince can be quite serious when it comes to reaching his goals. His stars also indicate a talent for leadership and decision-making—the right qualities for a future King!

Right: Tall and handsome, William says he chooses all of his own clothes and goes shopping for them by himself. **Opposite:** William jet skiing on a family getaway in St. Tropez in 1997. Friends say that even though he's basically soft-spoken and reserved, William has a bit of the daredevil in him and is always ready for a new adventure.

Camera Shy

It's well known that William often hates all of the attention he is paid and even threw himself on the floor of his father's car so he could avoid having his picture snapped at a polo match. Friends say he partially blames the press for the break-up of his parents' marriage and hates the idea that his mother was hounded by photographers until the day she died.

It started for William when he was just a little boy. He was snapped when he pinched one of his teachers and the press nicknamed him the "hooligan prince." During one family holiday years ago, William put up such a fuss about not wanting to appear in a group photo that he burst into tears when he was forced to pose. These days, William is always fussing with his hair, worried what it might look like in pictures. His friends say he hates to "look like a prat" (a jerk), so he will never wear a crash helmet when he is skiing and he always refuses to take off his sunglasses for photographers. Once, he tripped in front of a pack of paparazzi and he was utterly horrified that the pictures might actually be published.

Behind the scenes, William likes to put on shows with Harry for family and friends and was even caught singing "Nessun dorma," an aria from the Puccini opera *Turandot* at the top of his lungs for pal Tiggy. He knows that he will eventually have to face a lot of press attention without getting angry or lashing out.

During one trip to Switzerland before Diana's death, William even conducted his first "official" press conference with Harry and his young cousins Eugenie and Beatrice. Reporters wanted to know who the best skier was. Ever the diplomat, William said simply, "These two little girls are showing quite well."

SPICE MANIA

William attended the London premiere of *Spice World*, the movie debut of the Spice Girls. It was the first time William had ever appeared in public wearing a tuxedo. He looked smashing, of course! As he walked up to the door of the movie house at London's Empire Leicester Square, hundreds of girls started chanting, "We love you, William!" William just blushed a little bit and then started laughing. He got a bit of teasing from the group of friends he brought along with him, and little brother Harry thought it was pretty funny too.

There was a private meeting before the screening where the princes got to say hello to the Spice Girls. William blushed bright red when the girls all jumped on the chance to give him a hug. Harry had already met them during a visit to South Africa and he just smiled. The Spice Girls really enjoyed teasing Charles. They joked that he could be their new manager and he said he was "too expensive." Emma, also known as Baby Spice, said that she was thrilled to meet William and like millions of other girls she just wanted to say hi. "I really have a soft spot for Prince William," she told reporters. "It's a pity he's too young for me. And Harry told us, 'I'm going to tell all my friends to come and see this film,' which is really nice."

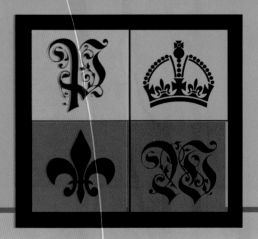

Hearts melted everywhere when William was seen wearing
a tuxedo for the very first time at the *Spice World* premiere
in London.

Prince
WILLIAM

CONCLUSION

Only time will tell what lies in Prince William's future. When will he inherit the British throne, and what kind of King will he be? Whom will he marry? The British people have high expectations for him and have already expressed their faith in him as a future leader. His good looks and charisma haven't hindered his growing popularity, either. He sends teenage girls' hearts aflutter and instills hope and faith in an expectant nation. Slowly and gradually, his life is being taken over by Buckingham Palace and by his grandmother, Queen Elizabeth. He has to learn throughout the years what it takes to become a monarch. Formal training for his future job as King will begin when he is eighteen, but already he has a sense of the destiny that is ahead of him. William once told both of his parents that he didn't want to be King, but now he is showing signs of being willing and able to assume the role to which he was born.

Royal watchers say that William has inherited his mother's good looks and his father's sense of duty. "He knows what the world will expect from him and is preparing himself for the big day."

BIBLIOGRAPHY

Adler, Jerry and Foote, Donna. "Growing Up Without Her." *Newsweek* (September 15, 1997): 50-53.

Arnold, Chuck. "Chatter." *People* (September 30, 1997): 10.

Kerr, Jane. "It Reminds William of His Mum and Dad's Love." *The Mirror* (October 30, 1997): 3.

Gleick, Elizabeth. "The Man Who Would Be King." *Time* (September 15, 1997): 43-47.

Halden, Rupert. "Happy 16th Birthday Prince William." *OK Magazine* (June 26, 1998): 24-26.

Haley, Larry. "Heartbroken Sons Have Their Mother's Courage." *National Enquirer* (September 23, 1997): 26-27.

Hoffman, Bill. "Di's in His Prayers As Wills Turns 16." *New York Post* (June 22,1998): 16.

_____. "Young Prince to March in Procession." *New York Post* (September 3, 1997): 8.

Hubbard, Kim. "Crown Jewel." *People* (June 6, 1998): 56-59.

Hutchinson, Bill. "Diana's Dying Words: 'Take care of my children.'" *Boston Herald* (September 11, 1997): 1, 4.

Johnson, Paul. "Why I Believe That William Should Be Our Next King." *Daily Mail* (January 7, 1997): 12.

Kay, Richard. "Farewell to the Palace of Memories for Princes." *Daily Mail* (February 7, 1998): 9.

"Losing Mom." *People* (September 15, 1997): 61-65.

McPhee, Michelle and Helen Kennedy. "Royal Family Finally Shows." *New York Daily News* (September 5, 1997): 6-7.

Plummer, William. "Loving Legacy." *People* (September 22, 1997): 88-95.

"Prince of Wales." *Ok Magazine* (April 3, 1998): 12.

Rae, Charles. "Brave Boys: Princes All Smiles at First Xmas Without Mom." *The Sun* (December 26, 1997): 29.

Reisfield, Randi. *Prince William: The Boy Who Will Be King.* New York: Pocket Books, 1997.

Rooke, Tim. "50 Most Beautiful People." *People* (May 11, 1998): 12.

Ross, Rory. "Is the Royal Family Letting It's Heirs Down?" *Tatler* (September 12, 1998): 115-118.

Singleton, Don. "William Should Be the Next Monarch, Poll Says." *New York Daily News* (January 10, 1997): 19.

Tumposky, Ellen. "Behind His Mum?" *New York Daily News* (September 3, 1997): 7.

Vickers, Hugo. "A Look Behind the Scenes of Prince William's Confirmation." *Hello* (July, 1, 1997): 25.

Wade, Judy. "In The Run-up to His 15th Birthday: Prince William." *Hello* (May 28, 1997): 66-67.

_____. "The Boy Born to Be King Turns 16." *Hello* (May 27, 1998): 10-18.

PHOTO CREDITS

Agence France Presse/Corbis-Bettmann: p. 11

All Action/Retna: ©Jonathon Furniss: p. 58; ©Anwar Hussein: p. 67; ©O'Brien/Peters: pp. 92-93; ©Doug Peters: p. 87

Alpha/Globe Photos, Inc.: pp. 5, 9, 26, 27 top, 28, 34, 42 top, 42 bottom, 43, 61, 72, 94; ©Jim Bennett: pp.21 right, 24; ©Randolph Caughie: p. 59; ©Richard Chambury: pp. 49, 56; ©Dave Chancellor: pp. 41, 53, 73 bottom, 77, 79, 91; ©Steve Daniels: pp. 22, 65, 69

AP/Wide World: pp. 10, 12, 13 bottom, 39; ©Hans Deryk: p. 50; ©Frank Gunn: p. 64

Camerapress/Retna Ltd. USA: p. 19, 20, 66, 78; ©G. Barlow: p. 18; ©Lionel Cherrault: p. 15, 16-17; ©S. Djukanovic: p. 30; ©Richard Gillard: pp. 2, 71, 74, 75; © Tim Graham: pp. 14, 47; ©Glenn Harvey: pp. 21 left, 27 bottom, 31, 32, 35, 38 bottom, 46; ©Stewart Mark: pp. 40, 45, 51 bottom, 82, 90; ©Scotsman: pp. 80-81

©Dominique Charriau/Stills Press Agency/ Retna: p. 84

Express Newspapers/Archive Photos: pp. 13 top, 33, 36, 52, 54, 86

©Glenn Harvey/ Globe Photos, Inc.: p. 51 top

Popperfoto/Archive Photos: p. 48

Reuters/Archive Photos: p. 60; ©Paul Hackett: p. 73 top; ©Jeff J. Mitchell: p. 57; ©Jeff Vinnick: p. 62-63, 83

Reuters/Corbis-Bettmann: pp. 29, 37

© Rex USA Ltd.: pp. 8, 25, 55, 86; ©Jim Bennett: 38 top, 88; ©Tim Rooke: pp. 7, 68, 71, 85; ©Stuart Newsham: p. 23

Solo Syndication/Archive Photos: p. 76

INDEX